Adult Gymnastics Workouts

More than 50 Gym and Weight Room Plans for
Physique and Safety

Definitions/abbreviations
BB: Barbell
DB: Dumbbell
HST: Handstand
OH: Overhead

Gymnastics Equipment
Ankle Weights
Circular Band
Bungee (tied with ankle size loops at each end)
Floor Bar
Jump Rope
Roll Bar or equivalent
Slider or Frisbee

Weight Room Equipment
Agility Ladder
Barre Ball
BB variety
Cardio Choices
DB variety
Jump Rope
Weight Ball
Yoga Ball

Colors
RED: Legs, hips to toes
BLUE: Arms, including shoulders and upper back
YELLOW: Abs, and other core
ORANGE: Lower Back, and stability
PURPLE: Compound Movements

Workouts

Gymnastics: 25 Minutes

Gymnastics: 15 Minutes and Less

Weight Room: 45 Minutes

Gymnastics A

Every Other (Abs and Legs)

2X:

1 Mat push
15 Ab roller
1 Min resi jump
15 Plank to squat with slider

1 Mat push
30 Hollow rocks
1 Min resi jump
30 seconds Plank on stability ball

1 Mat push
15 Leg lifts
1 Min resi jumps
20 lemon squeezers (tuck ins)

30 Kicks Swings all 3 ways (ankle weights)

Gymnastics B
Armnastics

2X:
1 Rope Climb
1 slider push up body push down and back
15 triceps dips
10 pullovers
5 Handstand walk up to panel (each hand leading)

3X:
20 bouncy cast trainer
20 Handstand Shrugs
5 Bar stalders
15 Handstand push ups

30 Kicks lifts all 3 ways (bungee)

Gymnastics C
Beam Team Legs (and abs)

3X:

15 Single leg jump backs (back handspring drill to resi)
15 Beam squat to stand (forward facing in beam feet)
15 Beam relevé (in passé, each foot)

3X:

1 min fast foot taps
1 min rebound up and town panel mat height
20 Box jumps
15 low beam leg explode jumps

3X:

30 Rocks hollow, arch, each side
30 lemon squeezers (tuck ins)
30 single leg V-ups

30 Kick pulses all 3 ways

Gymnastics D
Overtime Arms (and Back)

2 rounds 1 Min ea

Wall press handstand
Face down middle press position arms (up and down)
Overhead bungee pull (loop bungee to stationary object)
Mermaid lifts on vault table
Beam Pushups
Seated straddle side reaches
        (around the world hips up)
Single arm hang (split time in half for each arm)

30 rond de jambe hip high both legs (Forward to back)

Gymnastics E
Back to Basics

2X 10 each

1. Back Handspring over barrel
2. Front Handspring over barrel
3. Handstand forward roll
4. Cartwheel good side
5. Cartwheel bad side
6. Bridge kickover
7. Back tucks (any place/modify)
8. Backward roll
9. Front tucks (any place/modify)

30 Kick Swings all 3 ways (reclined, bungee)

Gymnastics F
Active Core

3X

20 second Mermaid Flutter on vault table

10 Windshield wipers

10 Bar hanging sit ups

8 hop inch worm with roll bar

3X

10 second mermaid hold on vault table

3 ea direction Plank 360 barrel roll

20 sec Elevated side plank (bottom leg in passé)

20 Hollow Hold

30 sec kick holds all ways (standing)

Gymnastics G
Don't Forget to Kick (and Arms)

2X

    10 Pullovers
    15 Alligators open close hang
    Front support walk side to side
    10 HST fall to planche w/ floor bar
    15 Leg lifts (last 30 degrees only)

2X

    10 Fish hang swings
    10 Back ext roll down hill
    10 Dips
    10 Elevators
    Hanging alternating grip change

2X

    20 FWD kicks elevated hips feet on block (lay)
    20 Back kicks in plank
    20 Sidekicks from side plank
    20 Passé pull with band

Gymnastics H
Must Rehab (Wrist/Ankle)
Jump rope 5 min

2x 30 sec
> Incline calf raise (each side, straight leg)
> Incline calf raise (each side, bent leg)
> Side to side over block rebounds (hands on a mat)

2x 30 sec
> Side to side sliding weight push each foot
> Single leg rebounds (other leg assist stability)
> Bungee toe points

30 ea X2
> Wrist push ups
> Foam squeeze
> Reverse finger lift topped w ankle weight
> Small DB wrist lift all sides
> Dowel wrist curl up (or roll bar)

30 Kick lifts all 3 ways (from kneel, ankle weights)

Gymnastics I
Weights and Bands

3x15 ankle weights
>   Walking kicks FSB
>   Bridge kicks
>   Down dog kicks
>   Passé lifts
>   Bungee on hips jump forward (attach to pole)

2X
>   10 Vertical leg fall side (laying down torso twist)
>   Side hollow crawl
>   Crab walk
>   15 x 3 point yoga knee plank (cross/nose/elbow)
>   15 Plank opposition leg/arm raise

Pike Walk
Split stretch

Gymnastics J
Fly High

Ankle weights:
- 3 x 10 each side
  - Cartwheel from knee
  - Modified Aerials
  - Tick Tocks

3x15
- High bar hanging split ups
- High bar hanging shuffle over and back
- Panel straddle up

2x10
- Rolling 360 bridge
- Pike slide through straddle
- Rolling splits

30 Seated Fan kicks Clockwise and Counterclockwise
Tramp Jumps

Gymnastics K
Dance Focus

Feet warm up
> Flex/point, forced arch, ankle circle, toe under stretch
> 20 relevé 5 ballet positions
> 20 demi plié 5 ballet positions
> 20 grande plié 5 ballet positions

2x

> 10 Single leg backward jump to stick (slow ea leg)
> 12 Hamstring curl fall down
> Floor routine ankle weights on ankles
> Beam routine ankle weights on wrists

2x15

> Hollow Rock
> Arch rock
> Side rock
> Arch hollow HST board bounce
> Plank board bounce

10 x FWD/Side ea leg resistance splits barrel or slider

30 Swinging Leg Kicks each side (ankle weights)
10 min Leaps/Jumps/Turns

Gymnastics L
Panel series

10 minutes over 5 panels
> Rebounds
> Long jump
> Single leg
> Frog

> Straddle mini press
> Push up ea side
> Squat on
> Sideways pike walk

2X 30 sec ea
> Fast Tap
> Step up (2 panel)
> box jump (3 panel)
> stairs
> sprint

30 Kick Lifts all 3 ways (bungee)

Gymnastics M
Slider Core

2X20
2 Plank Fan hand walk (180, feet on slider)
Slider elevated pike to rev plank
Slider plank to pike w floor bar
Slider lunge to stand
Slider Slide outs Hollow plank to flat

2X20
Between 2 Panels:
Hollow to straight body
Arch to straight body
Side arch to straight body both sides

30 Kick Pulses each way (kneeling)

Gymnastics N
Handstands and More

2 rounds 1 Min ea

Punch stalder up handstand

Single arm hang (split time in half for each arm)

Floor routine with weights on wrists

Piked push ups

Handstand walk

Forward raise with floor bar

Plank to wall HST stomach facing wall

30 rond de jambe hip high both legs (Arabesque to forward)

Olympic Warm Up
30 Minutes

5 Minutes:
Variation of run/squat/jump/jump rope
Relevé/heel/foot sides/walking

8 counts or 1 pass:

Head and wrist rolls
Shoulder circles
Arm swings Up, Down, Cross
Trunk twists
Toe/Foot Stretches
Ball of foot lifts
Top of toe lifts

Cardio:
Running
Forward runs
Backward runs
Knee Lifts
Butt kicks
Prance, toes point, legs straight
Power skips using big arm swing
2 steps rebound
2 steps pike walk 2 steps relevé

Standing Stretching:
Pilé twist lifting Leg
Hip push
Hip circle
Lean, hand on hip
Forward lean
Backward lean
Standing Straddle stretch (hands knees)
Arms through legs then thrust up
overhead
Alternating arm lifts, body bent over,
hand on floor
Standing pike (add legs crossed)

https://usagym.org/women/elite/coaching/

Floor Stretching:
Join legs in pike stand
Pike, squat, pike, squat, add quick toe
rises
Tuck roll to pike lay
Pike sit stretch with toes pointed
Pike sit stretch with toes flexed
Straddle legs, RL reach
Middle reach
Seal stretch
Quad stretches,

Feet:
Sit on knees
Lift body over top of toes
Achilles and calf stretch

Splits:
Stride stand, chest to knees
Deep lunge back leg straight
Knee on floor, pull L foot to from
behind to hip (quad stretch)
Lean forward to hamstring stretch
Slide to split
Bridge
Tuck and roll

Conditioning:
Straight jump
Tuck jumps
Crunches
V-ups
Arch ups
Push-ups
Rebounds

Kicks:
Forward, ¼ turn side, ¼ turn arabesque,
¼ turn repeat other leg
Walking needle kick

Bare Necessities Warm Up
10 Minutes

1 pass:
1. Run with arm circles
2. Skips
3. Chassé
4. 3 Rebounds to Stick Finish
5. Relevé Walks
6. Forward Kick + Arabesque Kick
7. Knee lunge to Lever
8. Full Turns
9. Handstands
10. Cartwheel to Relevé Steps Back

8 each or 8 second hold:
1. Torso Twist, knee circles
2. Throws and Windmills
3. Standing Pike (+cross leg)
4. Around the World in Straddle, rest in frog stretch
5. Reclined Kicks
6. Pike Sit
7. Wrist/Neck/Ankles circles, mini punch to ½ HST
8. Melting Heart (+thread needle)
9. Split Series (ea leg lunge, hamstring stretch, split)
   a. Hollow Rocks
   b. V-ups
   c. Arch Lifts
   d. Candle + Jump
   e. Tuck Jumps
10. Bridge Shoulder Rocks, Bridge Kicks

Gymnastics #1
Just Vault
15 Minute Warm up

1 runway pass:
Skips
High knees
Bottom kicks
Deer Run
Straight leg forward kick run
Straight leg backward kick forward run
Single leg hop right
Single leg hop left
Skips for height
Skips for length
Long jump
Bunny Hop
Sprint

Handstand shrug
Handstand hops
Star Cartwheel
Star Cartwheel with repulsion
Hop to stick finish

10 arm circle jumps on board
10 Backward jumps from board
10 Handstand bounces on board
10 Heel drives on table
10 Single leg jumps from elevated higher leg
         (Standing parallel to mat or low beam)

5 3-tier Jump to table jump down (panel, block, table)
5 Handstand fall flat on to 8"
5 Front Handspring off table to stick
5 Back tucks from table to stick

Gymnastics #2
Just Bars
15 Minute Warm Up

1. 2X
> 3 straddle glide swing
>
> 3 pull ups
>
> 1 pull over
>
> 3 casts
>
> 1 back hip circle dismount

2. 2X
> Kip
>
> 3 front hip
>
> 1 basket kip
>
> 1 Squat on jump to high bar

3. 2X
> 5 high bar tap swings
>
> 1 high bar pull over
>
> 5 dips
>
> 5 elevators
>
> 3 tuck toes to bar from hang
>
> 1 skin the cat to release dismount

4. 2X
> 10 Floor bar bounce trainer casts
>
> 5 Floor kip drill (roll bar or between 2 panel mats)
>
> Inverted hanging pike (5 swings optional)
>
> Hanging straddle (5 swings optional)
>
> 5 Hanging chin up leg lift
>
> 10 straight arm bungee pull downs

Gymnastics #3
Just Beam

15 Minute Warm up

Front Support Hold 10 sec

Feet:
10 Beam feet relevé
    each side
10 Beam feet relevé
    each side
    demi plié
10 Relevé in 5th
    each side
10 Sideways relevé
Développé
    from fwd passé
Développé
    from side passé
Forced arch stretch
steps
Toes under stretch steps
Ankle roll steps

1 Beam pass:
Walk forward relevé
Walk backward relevé
Grapevine
Side pivots in standing
relevé straddle
    (star body)
Passé forward Side
forward
Ice cream Scoop

to passe
High kicks forward
    To lock
Kneeling lunge
    to forward kick
Arabesque lifts
Lever walks
    to lunge finish
Forward pivot
    step, step
    backwards pivot
½ snap turn in passé
    + pivot
Squat to Stand
Three leg swing step

Jumps:
High jumps
Long jumps
Backward jumps
Bunny hops
Single leg hops

Dismounts:
3x Run stick dismount
3x Backward jump to
stick dismount

Gymnastics #4
Just Floor
15 Minute Warm Up

1 pass each

Tumbling:
Kick to Handstands good leg/ bad leg
Cartwheel step in to hollow
Cartwheel bad leg
Handstand walk
Power hurdle
Run to hurdle
Round off Rebound (from 1 step)
Handstand bridge kick over (modify as needed)
Backward Roll to Handstand or push up
Dive Roll
Dive Cartwheel

Dance:
Full Turns
Leaps in a Row (Repeat bad leg)
Chassé Leap Strait Jump (Repeat bad leg)
Strait Jump Tuck Jump
Sissonne good leg
Sissonne bad leg

Cross Tumbling (2 passes):
Aerials
Round off backhandspring
Round off two backhandspring
Front handspring step out, front handspring step out
Front handspring step out to round off or bounder
Front tuck progression
Back tuck progression

Gymnastics #5
Just Trampoline
15 Minute Warm Up

Hands and knees bound with tight core
Push up body bounce
Forward Peanut Rolls
Backward Peanut Rolls
Donkey kicks
Seat Drop
Knee Drop

Jumping Jacks
Forward Backward bounce
Side to side
Single Leg hops
Single Leg Hops Straight leg in front (both sides)
Single Leg Hops in arabesque (both sides)

Jump full turn both ways
Tuck Jump
Straddle Jump
Pike Jump
Right Split
Left Split
Switch Jump good leg
Switch Jump bad leg

Handstand Hops
Bounder Round off
Back Handspring
Front Handspring
Front Tuck
Back Tuck

Quick Conditioning (10 Minute Max)

10 each:

Press Handstands (modify)

Handstand Push-ups

Pike ups

Cast Handstands

Pull-overs

Levers

Rope Climb (1)

Leg lifts

Around the world stretch

Wall Handstand

Upper body Trunk Lift (feet under mat)
    Hollow, arch, RL sides

Lower Body Double leg lift (hold post)
    Hollow, arch, RL sides

https://usagym.org/women/elite/coaching/

Weight Room 1
Legs Now

5 Min bike
1 Running Lap

3X
10 Pulley Squats
15 Glute Bridges
8 ea Press squat bar from an angle squat to extension
8 Leg Press Main

3X
15 Arabesque lift with weighted ankle (isolate glute only)
30 Jumping jacks weighted
12 Quad ext
12 Glute Curl

Weight Room 2
Back to Back

5 Min Row

3X
15 Upright Fly
15 Face down fly
10 Heavy Row pulls
20 Arch up

3 Minute Row Machine

3X
15 Horizontal hang reverse leg lift (isolate glute)
15 Ab cable pulldown with rope
20 Reach to toes laying on back legs up the wall

3 Minute Row machine

3X
10 Push ups ea side on stationary weight ball
10 Dip machine
10 Pull ups
10 Tricep dips

Weight Room 3
Strong Wo/man

2X with 25 lbs plate, 1 minute each exercise

Ground touch to overhead extension
Biceps curl
Squat
Deadlift
Standing bent over row
Sit ups (no plate)
Farmer carry with (2) 25 lbs plates
      or overhead hold with (1) 25 lbs plate

Weight Room 4
Cardio Push

5 Min elliptical

2X20
Back/ab machine
Twisted side crunch or side V up
Preacher curl
Tricep OH extension

5 min Row

2X20
High knees
DB in feet hamstring curl
Leg Press machine Seated upright

5 min elliptical

2X20
Candle up
Suitcase Crunch
Butterfly Crunch
Hip lift off yoga block elevation

5 min Row

Weight Room 5
Major lifts

4X increasing weight decreasing reps 20, 15, 10, 5
Bench
Squat
Deadlift
Clean/jerk
Burpees

Weight Room 6

Shoulders/abs

5 min treadmill push

3X12

Bicycle sit ups
Reclined pike to candle up
Twist with BB
Hanging tuck side to side

3X10

Lateral raise with hand weights
Egyptian press forward
Upright press
Straight arm overhead shoulder 25 lbs plate

3X12

Hanging tuck ups
Sit ups on a declined bench
Trunk twist machine
Russian twist

3X10

Lateral raise with hand weights
Egyptian press forward
Upright press
Straight arm overhead shoulder 25 lbs plate

Weight Room 7
Surrender

3 minutes Row
3 minutes stairs

3x15
Surrenders
Single leg levers
Jump lunge switch
*Abs set

3X15
Glute curl (crawl shape, weight in back of knee)
Fire hydrant pee
Single leg squat on bosu balancer
*Abs set

3X
15 adductor pulls with band
30 Single leg heel raise
1 crab walk sideways with knees in band

3x (*between ea leg set)
30 V ups
30 flutter kicks
30 second plank

Weight Room 8
Barre Babe

5 Minutes elliptical

3x20
Barre ball standing clam
Barre ball glute lift
Barre ball ham squeeze

3x20
Seated Barre ball knee squeeze
Seated Barre ball abs squeeze
Seated Barre ball ham squeeze

3x20
Seated Barre ball toe taps side to side
Wall squat barre ball knee squeeze
Standing barre ball squeeze

Weight Room 9

Triathlon

        5 Min Treadmill or outdoor jog
        5 Min bike
        5 Min Row

        10 Min Treadmill or outdoor run
        10 Min bike
        10 Min Row

Weight Room 10
Paired Legs

3 Min elliptical
3 min stairmaster

3X10
Curtsy squat
Goblet Squat

3X10
Squat on
Side to side jump (20)

3X10
Kettlebell swing
Straight leg all to side 1 leg squat

3X10
Leg extension/Hamstring curl machines
Front to back jump (20)

3X 10
Arabesque kick with jump (ankle weights)
Seated Ad/Abduction machine

Weight Room 11
Chest vs. Back

5 Minute row machine

3x30 sec:
Figure 8 object behind back
DB Elbow butterfly
Prone Elbow touch forward
Lateral/FWD DB raise light

3X15
Lateral DB shoulder raise
BB bent over row
Forward DB shoulder raise

3X15
Pull ups
Dips
Tricep overhead extension

3X15
DB standing fly (bungee)
DB Renegade row in plank (band)
Bicep curl
Toe Raises (shins, 60)

3x30 sec (rehab)
Lateral shrug against wall
Dead bug arms on foam roller
Lateral to forward raise on foam roll
Foam roll up the wall shoulder ext

Weight Room 12
Full body

5 min elliptical

2x
30 sec easy style push ups
30 sec push up style shrugs

3X20
Step up with weight (height above knee)
Overhead plate circle
Wall ball squats (yoga ball between wall and back)

3X20
DB shoulder press
Single leg jump
Push ups on yoga block moving side to side
Rope pulls

3X20
 DB Bench Press
Tricep Dips
Egyptian forward press with plate
Horizontal trunk twist (machine or band)

Weight Room 13

Mixed HIIT

Bicycle 10 minutes

Reps: 20, 15, 10, 5 weight low to high

1. Mountain climbers (floor level)
2. Log roll + push up
3. Bicycle sit ups
4. TRX pull
5. BB glute raise
6. Side chase DB pickups
7. Battle rope vertical wave (1 min)

3 min bike

Weight Room 14
ABABAB Legs

2x2 Min ea
Incline Treadmill
Backwards Treadmill
Side shuffle

A:3X10
Sumo
Spazzo
Goblet

B: 3X10
Straddle stand dead lift BB
1 Cross floor weight push
Leg Press Standing

Weight Room 15
Arms Only

30x3
Incline push ups
Easy pull
Bungee all ways

3x10
Upright press
Opposition lateral raise
Crawl body DB in elbow skyward twist (ea side)

3x10
Biceps Curl
Bungee trunk twist
Push ups (diamond hands)

3x10
Pull up
Bench Press
Shoulder Lateral machine
Underhand BB pull

Weight Room 16
Plate and Body Weight

Run 5 laps

3x10 Wrist supported
1. Handstand shrugs
2. Handstand push ups
3. Handstand Shoulder taps

3x10 Plate
1. Double knee kneel plate extension
   (ground to overhead)
2. Oblique side bends
3. Drive steering wheel

3x10 Body weight
1. Squat jacks or full squat frog jumps
2. Flutter kicks in an arch
3. Side plank

3x10 Bungee or band
1. Hip flex knee lift
2. Trunk twist with bungee under kneeling knees
   (arms in opposition)
3. Ankle rehab/toe point

Weight Room 17
Shrug It Off

3 Min arm circles
3 Min leg swings
3 Min active yoga

> 3x15
> Hip to armpit DB pick up
> Shrug DB at sides
> Shrug DB oH
> Dip style shrug
>
> 3x15
> Standing bows
> Single leg balance circle OH press
> Lows back side reaches face down
>
> 3x15
> BB heavy glute bridge lift
> Sit down stand up no hands
> Thigh band reverse lifts
> Leg swing forward and back laying on side ankle weights

Weight Room 18
Uphill Both Ways

5 Min Treadmill Incline
5 Min elliptical
5 Min Stairmaster

10 Min Treadmill Incline
10 Min elliptical
10 Min Stairmaster

Weight Room 19
Hip Mobility

2x 15
Seated knees upright tap knees left center right
Hands free upright sit to stand feet outside hip distance
Sumo stretch to Right Left knee touch with 90 turn
Hands free upright sit to stand from cross leg

    1.20 Circles in front barre ball in bent knee

        3x15
        Bungee straight leg pull down
        Bungee arabesque pull down

    2. 20 Circles posterior barre ball in bent knee

3x15
        Barre or bosu frog 1/2 jump
        Pull up machine step down

    3. 20 Circle fan kick in front w ankle wt

  3x15
        Ankle weight bottom kick
        Knee to elbow w ankle weights

    4. 30 Circle fan kick posterior w ankle wt

Weight Room 20
Cardio Mashup

5 min row machine

2X15
Straight arm pulldown
DB bent over row
Bar tri pull downs
Weight ball vertical press

5 Min bike

2X15
Lat pulldown
Push ups on a yoga ball
Weight ball sit ups on a decline
Back extensions (mermaid)

5 Minute Stairmaster

2X15
Most muscular pose cable machine pull in
Forward press (cable machine)
Face down butterfly swim arm circles (light weight)
Calf press on leg press machine

Weight Room 21
Mountains to Sound

5 Min Elliptical

3x10
Swimmers
Opposite elbow to knee courtesy w/ DB press
Cross leg diagonal sit ups
Plank DB reaches (place DB Forward, side, diagonal)

3x10
Balanced box Step ups
Seal twist
Seal side to side reach

3x10
Mountain Climbers to elevation
Uneven bosu stand supported squats supported
Hands and knees core reach pull in
Hands and knees opposition lateral raise

Weight Room 22
Cardio Master

5 Min Bike

2x20
Deep squat from elevated surface
Fall to push up from knees
Single leg squat pickups
Upright rows

5 Min Stairmaster

2x20
Prone Weight ball throw
Upright ball overhead pass
Kettlebell Woodchoper
Battle rope lateral wave (1 min)

5 min bike

2x20
Jumping jacks DB
Supported BB glute bridge
Lunge switch

5 min Stairmaster

Weight Room 23
4x4 Legs

4x 30 sec
Ladder warm up
Bosu ball jump
Bosu balance
Bent leg calf raise

4x10
Long jump against bungee
Stand from deep seated squat
Frog squat to stand (knees together)
Glute leg ext machine

4x10
BB Front Squat
Grand plié
Jump down from elevation
Hamstring curl from face down

4x10
Hop from knees to stand
Single DB pick up
Plate lunge twist extend
Elevated straight leg glute bridge up

Weight Room 24
Thumbs Up for Tabata

3x1 min ea
    Weighted arm circles
    Shoulder rehab
    Upright vertical weight ball toss

3x20 ea 10 sec rest between exercises
1 min rest between sets

    Shoulder T thumbs up to OH
    Shoulder FWD thumbs up to OH

    Cross pull Reverse MM cables
    Serve from hip to extend outward 45 degrees

    Shoulder T thumps FWD to OH
    Shoulder FWD thumbs FWD to OH

    Shoulder fan against wall (foam roller optional)
    Wrist strength (small DB, Curl, side to side, reverse)

    Pike stretch to back extension
    Camel to upright on knees

Weight Room 25
Balance Life

3x20 warm-up
Knee stand with side side sit
1 arm reverse plank raises
Single Leg Modified Burpee to stand
Kneeling plate rotation left to right

3x20
Side glute standing leg lift
Seated single leg V-up
Inner thigh squeeze bungee

3x20
Ball squat against wall (squeeze core)
Gymnastics levers arms overhead
Glute bridge up (unstable surface)

3x20
Plank reverse kick up w/ ankle weight
Side plank top foot elevated bottom leg to meet
Knees side to side w/DB

Weight Room 26
The Twist

2x10

Plank, lift opposition foot slide through toe touch
(ea side)
Mountain climbers with twist
4 point plant circles (boys pommel horse)

3x12

Lunge w light OH DB twist
Single arm snatch to OH ext
Bungee twist w motion diagonal up
Bungee twist w motion diagonal down

3x12

Behind back small DB shoulder pass figure 8
Genie arms (overlapping elbow level) to vertical hands
Bow and arrow motion with band
Single arm row

3x12

Posterior single DB extension
Barre ball elbow squeeze
Knee lunge to yoga block balance
Arch hold with DB/band OH pull back

Weight Room 27
Cardio Playground

       5 min Ladder
       5 min Jump rope
       5 min Box Step Up

       10 min Ladder
       10 min Jump rope
       10 min Box Step Up

Weight Room 28
Legs, legs, legs Oh My!

5 min Treadmill Push

3x15
Single leg Dead
Straddle stance cross dead
Jump Rope 1 min

3x15
Frog Jump
Wide deep squat w plate
Jump from step up with leg swing (gainer drill)

3x15
Lunge to stand with single arm cable row
Jump and reach from lunge
Vertical jump w DB or ankle weights

Weight Room 29
The Old Ball and Cable Chain

5 Minute Treadmill Push

3x12 Yoga ball
1. Sit ups
2. Overhead hold reach back and touch wall
   (standing, glutes tight)
3. V ups with pass ball hands to feet to hands
4. Arch ups
5. Face down ball lift shoulder extension

3x12 Weight ball
1. Figure 8, standing
2. Sit ups laying with weight ball underback
3. Single leg ankle turn ins holding ball

3x12 Cable machine
1. Arabesque kick backs
2. Tricep pull backs
3. Rope bicep curl

Weight Room 30
Anger Management Pile On

1. 5 Push up
2. 4 Right Left duck and punch
3. 10 Sit up
4. 6 Ball slam
5. 30 sec Wall squat
6. 8 Tire flip
7. OH ball toss
8. 10 Briefcase pick up from negative

2 min kick box arms
   2 min Kick box legs

Weight Room 31
Doin' it

5 Min Jump Rope

3x10
Bear crawl Forward Sideways Backward
Push up with weight ball transfer
Pike Walk (hands to floor, straight legs)
Diamond hands HST Push up

3x10
Rope pull down
Weighted monster walk
Single leg Calf Raise

3x10
Egyption hold with twist
Bungee pull apart
Delt Raise

3x10
Reverse DB Raise
Tricep Dip
Tricep overhead extension

3 min Playground hang

Weight Room 32
HIIT Legs

10 minute Elliptical

10, 15, 20, 10

1. High knees with ankle weights
2. Side to side skater jumps (touch ground each side)
3. Candle stick to straight jump
4. Weight ball throw laying down
   (throw toward ceiling and catch)
5. Side step up jacks with 2 blocks plus jump squat
6. Single leg squat transferring side to side
7. Mountain climber plank jack combo

3 min elliptical

Weight Room 33
Curly Girl

10 Minute Elliptical

As Many Reps As Possible
3X light to heavy

Hammer curl
Wrist curl
Reverse bicep curl
Chin up from 45 degree hang (reverse grip)
Preacher curl

Crunch with hip lift
DB ham curl
Thrusters (Single arm DB or two hand BB)
Nose to knees hold

ABS for One Hundred Series
5x20 (Set to day of the Month)
Limit to 100 best technique

#1 Crunch (1st and 15th)
Crunch
Plank
Bicycle
Toe reach to touch
Hip lift

#2 Lemons (2nd and 17th)
Lemon squeezers
Knees side to side seated upright (weight optional)
V sit hold
Neutral hold and breath
Tuck rock hands free (Squeeze yoga block between knee)

#3 Barre (3rd and 18th)
Barre ball sit ups
Barre ball pulse
Barre ball squeeze
Barre ball seated upright taps
Supine ankle grabs

#4 Russian (4th and 19th)
Side sit ups twisted
Butterfly sit ups
Suitcase cross sit ups
Russian twist
Plank RL side

#5 Cross (5th and 20th)
Knee cross elbow, Nose, side in plank
Reclined knees fall side to side
Cat Cow (knee bungee optional)
Hip Circles on ball
Reclined breathing

#6 Star (6th and 21st)
Rainbow hollow hold
Side plank star body
Sideways tilted v up
Swish feet hollow hold
Right/left 90 degree leg tilt sit up

#7 Bug (7th and 22nd)
Reclined leg lifts on elbows
Wall straddle reach
Lean backs from seated upright
Crunch hold
Dead bug holding yoga ball with opposite knee/hand

#8 Roll (8th and 23rd)
Straddle open close from inverted pike
Glute Bridge with core focus
360 hollow arch hollow roll
Upright Bent knee circles
Backbend from knees or seated

#9 Cherries (9th and 24th)
Seated recline to upright posture with single DB at chest
Plank shoulder taps
Plank sideways walks rotating
Cherry pickers side to side
Arch up (chin and shoulders)

#10 Reach (10th and 25th)
Reclined alternating reaches upward
Side Bends w DB
Plank elbow to hands alternating
Prone hanging windmill
Tuck knee press iso hold

#11 Dip (11th and 26th)
Seated straddle leg lift
Plank Hip Dip
Seated pike lifts
Glute bridge knees touch side to side
Glute bridge hip tap

#12 Yoga ball (12th and 27th)
Yoga ball sit ups
Yoga ball back extension
Yoga ball supine lateral taps
Yoga ball tuck in
Yoga ball plank

#13 Saw (13th and 28th)
Stir the Pot
Row machine tuck in (feet on seat)
Plank jacks
Plank saw
Seated Straddle around the world reaches

#14 Dumbbell (14th and 29th)
Plank to down dog
DB extended arm OH circle
Supine sit up to pike with DB OH extension
Candle lower down

#15 Upside Down (15th and 30th)
Piked right to left over yoga block
Open close straddle over 2 yoga block
Yoga ball balance upright on knees (20 seconds)
Inverted pike to upright headstand
Inverted bicycle

#16 March Madness (31st of the Month)
Heavy DB OH high knee march
Kettlebell circle around waist
        (kneeling, touch floor diagonal with bell ea side)
Single leg stand kettlebell knee to elbow twist
Kettlebell pass under alternating knee (squat)
Glute bridge March

Types of Workouts
Mix it Up!

1. Circuit Training. *15-20 reps* at a moderately fast tempo of *4-6 full body exercises.* (20-30 seconds rest). *3-6 circuits.*

2. Pyramid. *a) Ascending pyramid: b) Descending pyramid: c) Triangle pyramid*
Reps or weight

3. HIIT – High Intensity Interval Training 50 seconds of work/10 seconds of rest

4. AMRAP – As Many Reps As Possible

5. Tabata *20 seconds* of work, *10 seconds* of rest. 4 minutes per set, 1 min rest between 4-5 rounds

6. Supersets. Pairs of exercises that are done back-to-back before moving on to the next pair of exercises.

7. EMOM – Every Minute On the Minute. Complete a specific number of reps every minute

8. Pile On. Each set add another exercise

9. Max

10. 5 x 5 Strength training *5 sets of 5 reps* heavy, limit 4-5 exercises

REHAB

Ankle:

    Towel toe scrunch

    Dice pick up

    Bungee up/down/Left/Right

    Yoga block balance

Wrist:

    Rice Bucket Circles and Open close grip

    Fry pan twist

    Flat bungee or sock open close

Shoulder:

    FWD and lateral raise

    Clam open close elbows

    Dead bug arms on foam roller

    Vertical reach with foam roller

    Simon says

    Door hinge w band

    90 degree bent elbow rotation

    Light weight circles

    Neck/pec/reach behind Stretch

Low back:

    Supine Abdominal Brace (flattening)

    Glute bridge

    Bird Dog reach

    Windmill (leaning)

    Upright monkey grabs

    Bungee crossed deadlift

    Hamstring machine hold stretch

    Plank

GOALS:

Jan	
Feb	
March	
April	
May	
June	
July	
Aug	
Sept	
Oct	
Nov	
Dec	

Year Goal:

Ten Things You Need to Know About Sports Nutrition

1. Look Beyond Weight When Determining Health

2. Building Muscle Takes More Than Just Protein

3. Protein: It's Not Just More, But When and How Much

4. Infrequent Meals Cause Problems

5. Fresh foods help the microbiome keep you healthy

6. Good Food, Bad Food, Wrong Choice

7. Relative Energy Deficiency in Sport (RED-S) can be a Problem

8. Poor Hydration, Poor Performance

9. Recovery from Exercise is Just as Important as the Exercise

10. It Is Important to Learn How to Lower Stress

AMERICAN COLLEGE of SPORTS MEDICINE, LEADING THE WAY

https://tinyurl.com/nutritionfactsblog

Hydration

- Make sure you drink plenty of fluids with every meal, whether or not you will be exercising.
- Drink about 16 ounces (2 cups) or 480 milliliters of water 2 hours before a workout. It is important to start exercising with enough water in your body.
- Continue to sip water during and after you exercise, about 1/2 to 1 cup (120 to 240 milliliters) of fluid every 15 to 20 minutes. Water is best for the first hour. Switching to an energy drink after the first hour will help you get enough electrolytes.
- Drink even when you no longer feel thirsty.

Calorie Approximations:
(May vary by age)

Women

100-130 lbs	2000
130-160 lbs	2200
160+ lbs	2400

*Add 100 Calories per day per intense hour of exercise

Men

110-150 lbs	2400
150-190 lbs	2700
190+ lbs	3000

*Add 100 Calories or more per day per intense hour of exercise

The American College of Sports Medicine recommends a range of 1.2-1.7 g protein/kg body weight per day for adults. Most research available right now points to a total protein requirement between 1.4 g/kg and up to 3.0 g/kg in some cases depending on training goals and health status

Daily Protein Need:
1. Wt. in lbs_____ X .45 = _____Wt. in kg

2. Wt. in kg _____ X 1.4 = _____ grams Protein Per Day

3. Grams protein per day _____ ÷ # meals and snacks per day = Protein goal per sitting _____

Examples of 20 Grams of Protein
(Great for main meals)

Meat:
    4 oz. Chicken, Steak, or Fish
    ½ cup Ground Turkey
    ½ can Tuna
    6 Jumbo Shrimp

Vegetarian:
    3 Large Eggs
    ¾ cup cottage cheese

Vegan:
    2 Scoops Orgain Vegan Protein Powder
    ⅓ Block Firm Tofu (½ Block soft/silken)
    1 cup Lentils
    2 cup Edamame (Shell on)
    1 cup Edamame (Shelled)
    ½ cup dry roasted soybeans
    ⅓ block Tempeh
    1 Patty Beyond Burger

Foods with 8-10 grams protein per serving:
(To be used as snacks, combo of 2 for main meal, or as an add on to main meal)

    8 oz Milk or yogurt
    1 oz Cheese
    ½ can refried beans
    ½ cup hummus
    ½ cup black beans

2 Tbsp nut butter
¼ cup nuts
¼ cup pumpkin seeds (no husk)
2 Tbsp hemp hearts

High Protein Grains (5-7 grams)
½ cup Quinoa
½ cup wild rice
½ cup steel cut oats

More Sports Nutrition information found at
https://www.acsm.org/education-resources/trending-topics-resources/nutrition

https://www.nutrition.gov/topics/basic-nutrition/eating-exercise-and-sports

https://www.eatrightpro.org/practice/dietetics-resources/sports-nutrition-and-athletic-performance

Workout Check Off

2025 CALENDAR

JANUARY

S	M	T	W	T	F	S
			1	2	3	4
5	6	7	8	9	10	11
12	13	14	15	16	17	18
19	20	21	22	23	24	25
26	27	28	29	30	31	

FEBRUARY

S	M	T	W	T	F	S
						1
2	3	4	5	6	7	8
9	10	11	12	13	14	15
16	17	18	19	20	21	22
23	24	25	26	27	28	

MARCH

S	M	T	W	T	F	S
						1
2	3	4	5	6	7	8
9	10	11	12	13	14	15
16	17	18	19	20	21	22
23	24	25	26	27	28	29
30	31					

APRIL

S	M	T	W	T	F	S
		1	2	3	4	5
6	7	8	9	10	11	12
13	14	15	16	17	18	19
20	21	22	23	24	25	26
27	28	29	30			

MAY

S	M	T	W	T	F	S
				1	2	3
4	5	6	7	8	9	10
11	12	13	14	15	16	17
18	19	20	21	22	23	24
25	26	27	28	29	30	31

JUNE

S	M	T	W	T	F	S
1	2	3	4	5	6	7
8	9	10	11	12	13	14
15	16	17	18	19	20	21
22	23	24	25	26	27	28
29	30					

JULY

S	M	T	W	T	F	S
		1	2	3	4	5
6	7	8	9	10	11	12
13	14	15	16	17	18	19
20	21	22	23	24	25	26
27	28	29	30	31		

AUGUST

S	M	T	W	T	F	S
					1	2
3	4	5	6	7	8	9
10	11	12	13	14	15	16
17	18	19	20	21	22	23
24	25	26	27	28	29	30
31						

SEPTEMBER

S	M	T	W	T	F	S
	1	2	3	4	5	6
7	8	9	10	11	12	13
14	15	16	17	18	19	20
21	22	23	24	25	26	27
28	29	30				

OCTOBER

S	M	T	W	T	F	S
			1	2	3	4
5	6	7	8	9	10	11
12	13	14	15	16	17	18
19	20	21	22	23	24	25
26	27	28	29	30	31	

NOVEMBER

S	M	T	W	T	F	S
						1
2	3	4	5	6	7	8
9	10	11	12	13	14	15
16	17	18	19	20	21	22
23	24	25	26	27	28	29
30						

DECEMBER

S	M	T	W	T	F	S
	1	2	3	4	5	6
7	8	9	10	11	12	13
14	15	16	17	18	19	20
21	22	23	24	25	26	27
28	29	30	31			

Notes:

Notes:

Notes:

Made in the USA
Monee, IL
28 August 2024

64754595R00044